Working Dogs

Sherry Shahan

This edition published in 2001.
Copyright © 1999 by Sherry Shahan.

Published by Troll Communications L.L.C.

Planet Reader is an imprint of Troll Communications.

Printed in the United States of America.   ISBN 0-8167-6522-7

10 9 8 7 6 5 4 3

For Shannon Lorrance—your very own book!

Welcome to Planet Reader!

Invite your child on a journey to a wonderful, imaginative place—the limitless universe of reading! And there's no better traveling companion than you, the parent. Every time you and your child read together you send out an important message: Reading can be rewarding and *fun*. This understanding is essential to helping your child build the skills and confidence he or she needs as an emerging reader.

Here are some tips for sharing Planet Reader stories with your child:

Be open! Some children like to listen to or read the whole story and then ask questions. Some children will stop on every page with a question or a comment. Either way is fine; the most important thing is that your child feels reading is a pleasurable experience.

Be understanding! Sometimes your child might need a direct answer. If he or she points to a word and asks you to tell what it is, do so. Other times, your child may want to sound out a word or stop to figure out a sentence independently. Allow for both approaches.

Enjoy! This book was created especially for your child's age group. Talk about the story. Take turns reading favorite parts. Look at how the photographs support the story and enhance the reading experience.

And most of all, enjoy your child's journey into literacy. It's one of the most important trips the two of you will ever take!

Big dogs.
Small dogs.
Dogs that
ride a school bus! What
kinds of dogs are these?

Dogs that love to work!
Skilak is a search-and-rescue
dog.
"Search!"

Skilak digs in the snow.

He finds the man.

"Good dog!"

Blackie and Fidel herd sheep.
They herd sheep into a pen.

It's time to spray the sheep for bugs.

Blackie gets sprayed, too!

Falcon is a police dog.

Is there something
bad in a box?

If there is,
Falcon will find it!

Long ago, Dalmatians had an important job. Fire trucks used to be pulled by horses. Dalmatians chased the horses to make them run faster.

Today these dogs don't chase fire trucks. Dalmatians are firefighters' special friends.

Tijo rides a bus to school.
He is a service dog.
He helps his owner do lots
of things she
can't do by
herself.
Tijo opens
doors.

"Get it!"
Tijo picks up a book.

Tijo worked hard today.
Now he gets to nap!

Sled dogs once pulled heavy loads over icy trails. Now dog teams run in races.

"Three, two, one
— mush!"

The Beagle
Brigade
works at
the airport.

Are there meats, fruits,
or vegetables in these
suitcases?

Sniff!
Sniff!
Get a
whiff?

Find it!

Relish is a Seeing Eye dog.
He helps his owner,
who is blind.

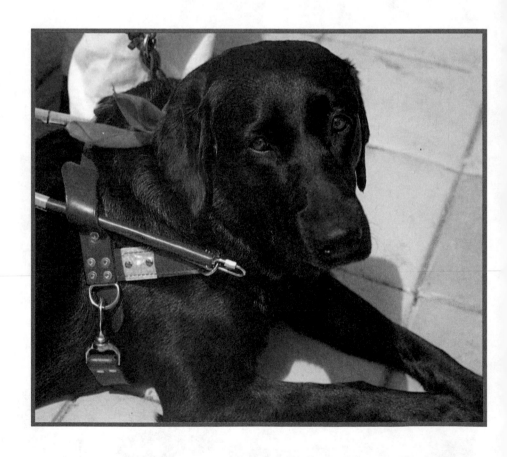

Relish leads the way
across a busy street.
Watch out for the curb!

Relish knows how to make friends, too.

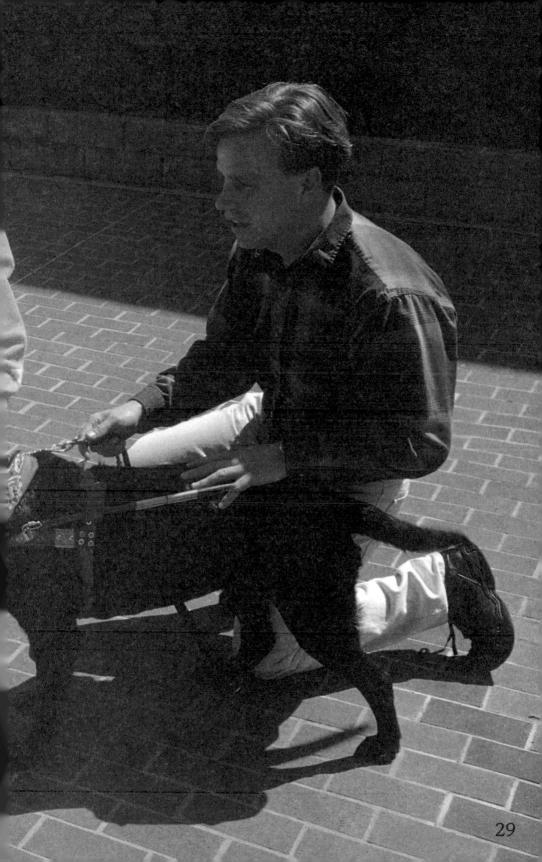

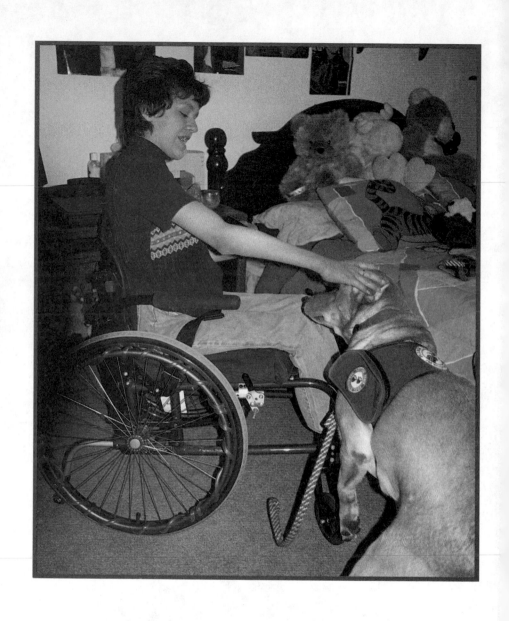

Working dogs love to be petted and praised.
Just like your dog!

INDEX